GIFTS
FOR
YOUR DOG

GIFTS FOR YOUR DOG
A READER'S DIGEST BOOK

Produced by Tucker Slingsby Ltd.

Copyright © 1995 Tucker Slingsby Ltd.

Library of Congress Cataloging in Publication Data

Gifts for your dog.
   p.   cm.
"A Reader's digest book"—T.p. verso.
ISBN 0-89577-793-2
1. Dogs—Equipment and supplies.
2. Handicraft. 3. Gifts.
I. Reader's Digest Association.
SF427.15.G54 1995
636.7'0887'028—dc20   95-9068

Illustrations by Roger Fereday
Step-by-step diagrams by John Hutchinson
Special thanks to Blair Brown Hoyt, Bob Mathias,
Cheryl Owen, and Sandy Ransford

Printed in Singapore

GIFTS
FOR
YOUR DOG

Reader's Digest

The Reader's Digest Association, Inc.
Pleasantville, N.Y. / Montreal

Contents

For Playful Puppies

Puppies look cute, but they are actually shrewd operators. Within seconds of entering your home, they'll demand armloads of play things, a comfy corner, warmth, and unending attention – and you'll find yourself surrendering to every whim.

Puppy Love

A new puppy is likely to feel a little lost and forsaken on first arriving in your home. You'll need to provide lots of toys, blankets, old pillows, and a host of chewable confections. And, if you'd rather not be forever picking up the ravaged remains of your Sunday shoes or favorite umbrella, you must take it upon yourself to teach your little bow-wow which chewable items are fair game and which are not! Remember to keep anything small enough to swallow well out of reach.

Box bed

A cardboard box for a bed will be heaven on earth to your pooch. A store-bought bed will get gnawed to shreds during teething. A box is also practical because when your puppy has an accident, it can be recycled in a flash.

Home comforts

To make your puppy's bed cozy, line the bottom with a washable blanket. For a personal touch, add appliquéd hearts or bones (see page 28).

That's my bowl

Of course, your puppy needs its own food bowl and water bowl. Follow the instructions on page 50 to decorate the bowls with appropriately enticing puppy motifs.

Toy time

Create a puppy playground with a cardboard box full of wonderful toys. Your local pet store will be able to supply the obligatory rubber bone. You can add an old shoe or slipper. Remove any shoelaces or buckles that might hurt your pup. Other favorites will be a plastic ball and an old teddy bear. Make sure everything is too large for your puppy to swallow.

Collar style

Your puppy will enjoy being grown up enough to wear a collar. Make sure it has a name tag giving your address and phone number. Choose a smart leather collar with a buckle so that the collar can be adjusted as your dog grows.

Heart to Heart

Most little pups on their first few nights in a new home miss their mommies and their litter mates. A loudly ticking clock, with its steady rhythm reminiscent of mommy's heartbeat, can provide the sought-after solace. You could just wrap any ticking clock securely in a blanket, but this friendly puppy-faced clock container makes a very special gift for a new puppy.

Materials Needed
- Stretch velvet:
  18 in. x 24 in.
- Polyester batting:
  9 in. x 36 in.
- Black felt: 6 in. square
- Black stranded cotton
  embroidery thread
- Velcro
- Basic sewing equipment
- Small clock with a
  loud tick

1 Cut four circles from the velvet, each with a 7 in. diameter. Cut two circles the same size from the batting. From the felt, cut two small circles for the eyes and a triangle for the nose.

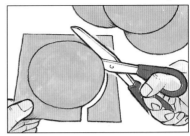

2 Pin the nose to the center of the right side of one velvet circle and pin the eyes midway between the nose and the top of the fabric. Hand sew the features very firmly in place. Embroider the mouth using stem stitch (see page 64).

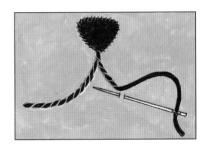

3 Baste one batting circle to the back of the face. Baste the second batting circle to the wrong side of one of the other velvet circles.

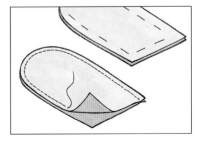

4 Trace the ear pattern (see page 13) and use it to cut out four velvet ears. Baste the ears together in pairs with right sides together. Stitch, using a ¼ in. seam allowance and leaving the straight end open.

11

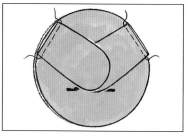

5 Clip the curves of the ears and turn right side out. Baste the ears in position on the right side of the face circle. Allow about 4½ in. between the ears, measuring around the top of the face circle.

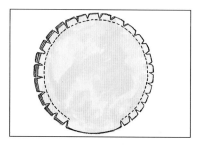

6 With right sides together, stitch each of the remaining velvet circles to a padded circle to make two "bags". Use a ¼ in. seam allowance and leave a 4½ in. gap on the lower edge of each. Clip the curves.

7 Turn the bag with the face right side out leaving the other bag as it is. Slip this bag inside the face bag and pin the two pairs of edges, right sides together, leaving an opening to insert the clock. Slipstitch the edges closed.

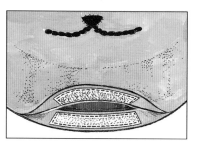

8 Fold the ears at each side of the face and hand sew securely in place. Sew Velcro to each side of the opening. Put in the clock and close.

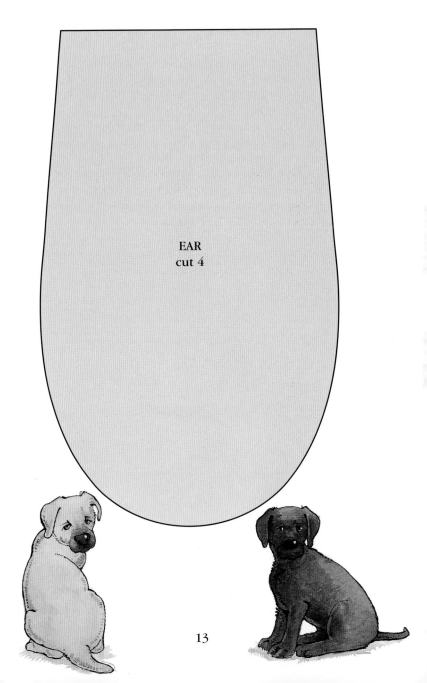

EAR
cut 4

13

Teddy Toy

All good puppies deserve their own teddy toy. This cute little character takes so little time to make that you can shower a deserving dog with a collection of bears in a rainbow of colors.

For a really tiny puppy, you can make the teddy the same size as the pattern. But, if there is any danger of puppy being able to swallow the toy, enlarge the pattern (see page 58). Sew string or elastic very firmly to the bear so you can drag it along the carpet to play energetic chasing games.

Materials Needed

- Felt: 9 in. x 36 in.
- Ribbon: 18 in. x 1 in. wide
- Fabric pen, black
- Polyester fiberfill
- Basic sewing equipment
- String/elastic: 36 in. x ½ in. wide (optional)

1 Trace around the bear shape (page 17) to make a paper pattern. To enlarge the pattern first, see page 58. Fold the felt in half and pin on the pattern. Cut out two shapes.

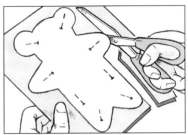

2 Pin the teddy bodies together and machine stitch using a ¼ in. seam allowance. Leave a 2 in. opening for turning.

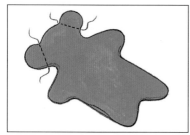

3 Clip curves and corners and turn right side out. Sew across bottom of ears as shown.

4 Using a fabric pen, draw eyes, nose, and mouth. Tie the ribbon into a bow and sew it very firmly to the front of the bear.

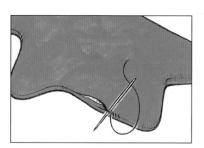

5 Stuff the bear with polyester fiberfill until it is soft. Do not overfill. Slipstitch the opening closed.

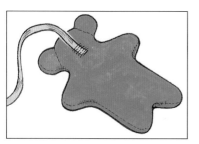

6 To pull the bear along the floor, stitch a length of string or elastic very securely to the back of the bear's head.

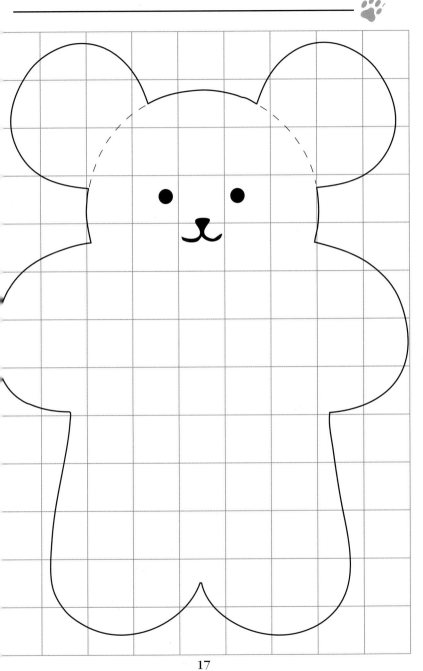

Warm Welcome

All pet dogs, little pups and big guys, will be yelpingly grateful for an occasional cuddle with a warm hot-water bottle. Instead of wrapping your bottle in a blanket that might fall off and leave your friend exposed to excessive heat or cold, why not go whole hog and make a hot-water bottle cover? This makes a distinguished, one-of-a-kind, welcome-home gift.

Materials Needed

- Cotton fabric:
  36 in. square
- Medium batting:
  18 in. x 36 in.
- Bias binding:
  80 in. x 1 in. wide
- 2 large snap fasteners
- Teacup
- Pencil, ruler, and
  felt-tip pen
- Basic sewing equipment
- Hot-water bottle

1 Draw four rectangles 14 in. x 10 in. on the cotton fabric. Draw two rectangles the same size on the batting. Cut out the six rectangles.

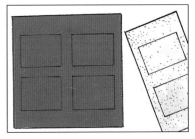

2 Place a teacup on a corner of one rectangle, then draw around the cup to make a curved corner. Repeat on the other corners. Cut around the curves. Repeat with the remaining rectangles.

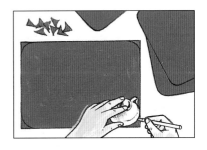

3 Place a batting rectangle on the wrong side of a fabric rectangle. Put a second fabric rectangle on top, right side out, to make a batting sandwich. Baste the layers together. Repeat with the remaining rectangles.

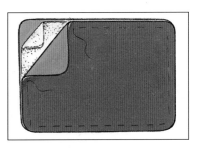

4 Measure 3 in. down the long sides of the fabric sandwich. Mark with a pin on both sides. Open out one edge of the bias binding. With right sides facing, stitch the binding along foldline to the upper edge between the pins.

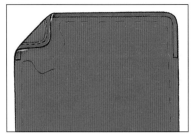

5 Fold the binding over to cover the raw edges and baste to the back of the sandwich. The folded edge should extend ⅛ in. beyond the seam. Machine stitch along the seam through all thicknesses. Repeat for the other sandwich.

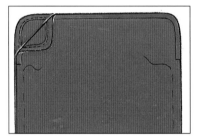

6 Place the sandwiches on top of each other and baste the raw edges together.

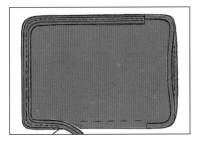

7 Open out one edge of the remaining binding and, from the front, stitch along the foldline around the raw edges on three sides. Turn under the ends of the binding at the start and finish.

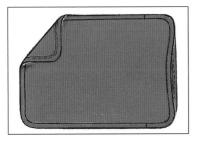

8 Fold the binding over to cover the raw edges and baste to the back with the folded edge extending ⅛ in. beyond the seam. Machine stitch through all thicknesses.

For Pampered Pets

Looking grrr-eat every minute of the day can be a tall order for even the most style-conscious canine. But with a little help from you and a small mountain of bows, barettes, bejeweled collars, and grooming tools, it's a cinch.

Fringe on Top

Breeds whose hair falls in their eyes can wear it pulled off the face for special occasions. If your dog looks good in ribbons and bows, keep a collection of attractive hair ornaments on hand to suit every social event.

Sweet and Simple

The simplest adornment of all is a piece of pretty ribbon. Check your local notions shop to see what's available – bearing in mind the subtleties of your canine's coloring, of course. Choose from spotted, striped, or checked ribbons for summer days. A velvet or richly embroidered ribbon is state-of-the-art for winter parties.

Securi-tie

If ribbons tend to slip out of your dog's hair, tie a separate bow and sew it onto a pony-tail

holder. Stitch through the knot of the bow and pass the needle around and through the holder to secure it.

Bejeweled

For a special event, sew *faux* pearl beads very securely to a pony-tail holder. Or, make a velvet bow and sew a sparkling jewel to the center. This kind of effect looks particularly good on little pooches with a taste for the extravagant. Don't risk them on uncool canines who may choose to chew them!

Flower Power

For an alluringly feminine effect put a green pony-tail holder in your dog's hair, then add a tiny bouquet of pretty silk flowers. Fresh flowers will look and smell great too.

Barettes

To jazz up plain barettes, personalize them using enamel paint. Create your own design, such as a row of little flowers, holly leaves and berries for Christmas, or your dog's name, initials, or a family crest.

Party Animals

When you include your pet in any suitable shindigs in your home, you will want to provide appropriate party wear. Put your pooch in a merrymaking mood with a custom-made collar. The creative owner will find fashioning a bow-wow tie or two is no trouble at all. Consider *soirée* black or shimmering gold *lamé* ribbon for the *au courant* canine – strictly for occasional indoor party wear, of course.

Materials Needed
- Stiff black or gold ribbon: 54 in. x 1 in. wide
- Snap fastener
- Basic sewing equipment

1 Measure the circumference of your dog's neck, allowing for a snug, but not tight, fit. Cut a piece of the ribbon about 4 in. longer.

2 Turn under raw edges and hem. Sew the snap in place on the ends of the ribbon. Check the fit. You should be able to insert two or three fingers between the collar and the dog's neck.

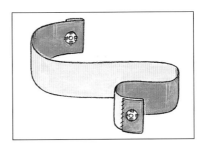

3 Make a ribbon bow. Stitch it securely to the collar. Leave it plain, or sew on fake jewels or pearls very securely. Be sure your dog doesn't get a chance to chew the collar!

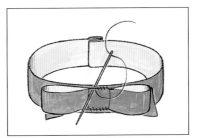

Pillow Talk

The dog-tired dog deserves a pillow to sleep on. This cushion is ideal for those doggies who expect a little luxury in their lives.

Buy a ready-made washable pillow form the right size for your dog's basket, favorite chair, or secret napping place. Pick a plain cotton fabric to cover it that will look good adorned with a big appliqué bone. Or, decorate it with an artistic selection of smaller, different-colored bones.

Materials Needed

- Purchased pillow form
- Cotton fabric for cover
- Cotton fabric for large bone: 12 in. square
- Double-sided fusable interfacing: 12 in. square
- Paper and pencil
- Basic sewing equipment

1 Cut out two squares or rectangles of fabric exactly the same size as the purchased pillow form. Do not be tempted to make the cover bigger than the pillow or it will be too big and make the pillow flat.

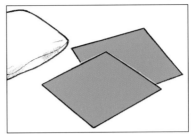

2 To make the motif, iron the interfacing onto the wrong side of the bone fabric. Trace the bone motif (page 60) onto the interfacing, enlarging it if desired. Cut out bone and peel off backing.

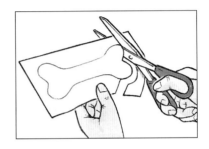

3 Pin the bone right side up onto the right side of one pillow cover piece. Fuse in position with an iron if desired. Machine or hand sew around the edges in satin stitch.

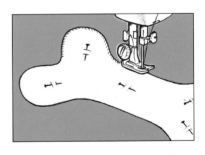

4 Pin the two pillow pieces right sides together. Sew around the edges, leaving an opening in one side. Turn right side out and insert pillow form. Hand or machine stitch the opening closed.

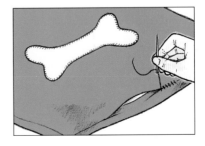

Grrr-ooming

When constructed of rough toweling on one side and silk on the other, a grooming mitten comes in mighty handy. The toweling side is ideal for giving a quick rub-down to remove loose hairs, dampness, or mud, while the silk side will make your pooch's coat gleam.

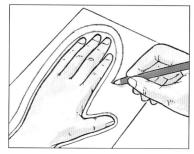

Materials Needed

- Silk fabric: 12 in. square
- Toweling: 12 in. square
- 1 sheet of paper a little larger than your hand
- Pencil
- Basic sewing equipment

1 Place your hand palm down, fingers together, on a sheet of paper. Draw around the hand and thumb and at least 4 in. down the wrist to make a mitten shape. Now draw a second outline 1 in. outside the first. Cut around the outside line.

2 Pin the paper pattern to the silk, draw around it, then cut out the mitten shape. Repeat for the toweling fabric.

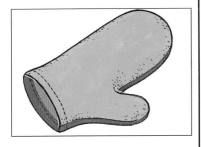

3 Pin the two pieces right sides together. Machine stitch around edges, using a ¼ in. seam allowance. Do not sew across wrist opening. Turn the raw edge over twice and hem. Turn mitten right side out.

Go for Gold

Every dog owner knows that a pet needs a customized grooming kit. For the ultimate luxury, paint your pet's initials or a personal motif on its brush and comb. Go for a lavish gold monogram for your canine-about-town, or try a brightly colored paw print for less sophisticated types.

Use non-toxic enamel paint. Freehand designs are limitless, or you can use the motifs on pages 58–63. To make a stencil, see page 51.

For Dogs About Town

With a stylish wrap, cozy travel rug,
and essential dog-u-ments all neatly filed,
the debonair dog about town
is ready for anything.

Dirty Doggy Bag

Sporting canines, who revel in mud-rolling and dirty puddles, will find this cozy terry cloth rub-down bag indispensable. Just pop a messy dog into this washable sack. It will keep your dog warm and dry, and the interior of your car will be free from mud and hairs.

The pattern comes in three sizes, so you're sure to get the right fit. The bag should be roomy and comfortable so your pet can stand and sit with ease. There's no pattern for teeny, tiny toy dogs as they can be coddled in your pocket when the going gets rough. Choose a dark color for your doggy bag so it'll show wear and tear less.

Materials Needed
- Terry cloth fabric:
  for large dog:
    40 in. x 68 in.
  for medium dog:
    34 in. x 48 in.
  for small dog:
    30 in. square
- Large snap fasteners:
  3–6 depending on size
- Pinking shears
- Basic sewing equipment

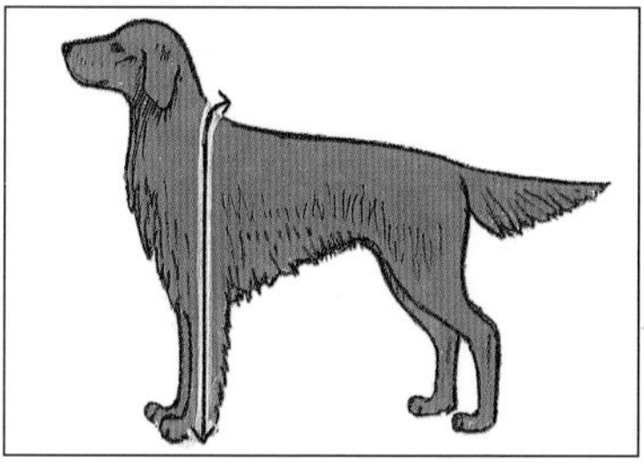

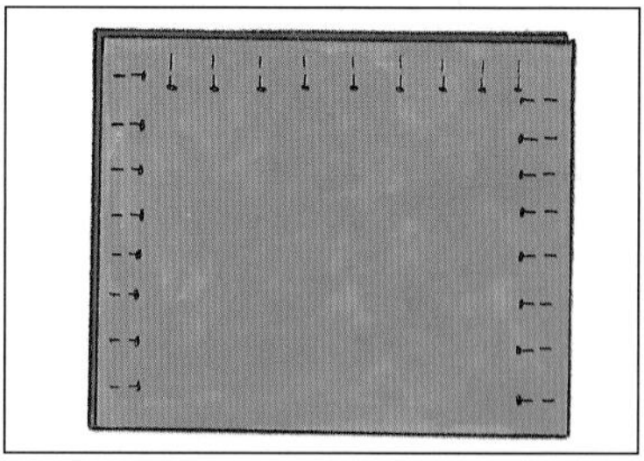

1 First measure your dog. When the dog is standing, measure from the front paw up the leg to the center of the back. If this measurement is less than 12 in., use the small pattern. If it is over 12 in. but under 20 in., use the medium pattern. Up to 28 in. qualifies as a large dog.

2 Cut the terry cloth to the correct size for your dog. Overcast or serge all the edges to prevent fraying. Fold the fabric in half and pin the sides and top together.

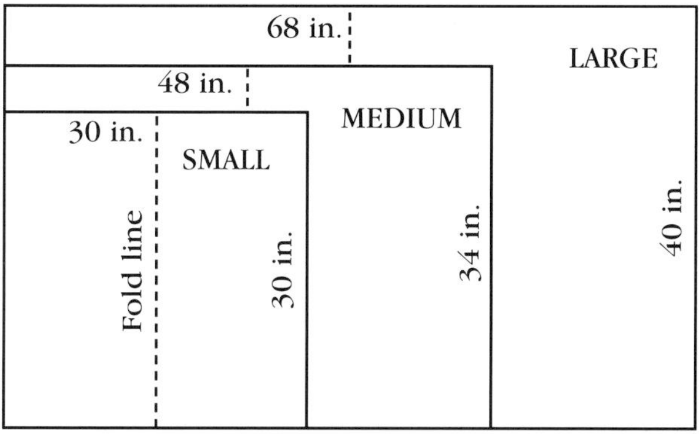
68 in.
LARGE
48 in.
MEDIUM
30 in.
SMALL
Fold line
30 in.
34 in.
40 in.

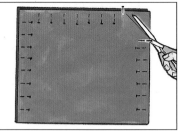 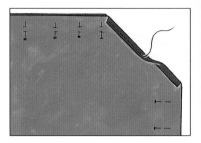

3 Using the appropriate size (see below), mark the position of point A with pins 1 in. from the raw edge. Cut away a triangle of fabric to make the neck hole. Cut through both thicknesses.

4 Fold over ½ in. on the neck edges and press. Fold over another ½ in. and machine stitch to hem.

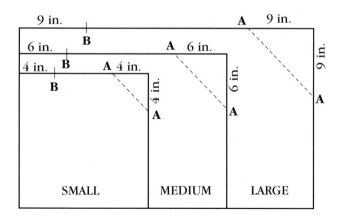

9 in.   A   9 in.

6 in.   **B**   A   6 in.

4 in.   **B**   A 4 in.

B

4 in.

6 in.

9 in.

A

A

A

SMALL   MEDIUM   LARGE

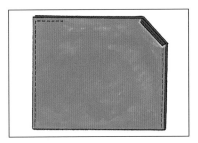

5 With right sides together, stitch along the front edge, using a ½ in. seam allowance. Sew along the tail end to point B, using a 1 in. seam allowance. Trim corners. Turn right side out.

6 Turn under ½ in. on top raw edges and press. Turn over another ½ in. and machine stitch to hem. Securely sew a row of large snaps along opening edges. Position snaps about 4 in. apart.

The Dog House

If your pooch lives in a plain dog house, you can turn it into a fanciful palace. Simply add a false front made from a single sheet of plywood and attach it to the kennel.

If desired, you can cut castle turrets and spires or simple rounded shapes. Colorful paints will dramatize your modish architecture. Decorate the façade with imposing battlements, graceful arches, glamorous windows, or a romantic balcony.

Materials Needed
- Plywood: at least 1 in. larger than overall size of front of kennel
- Scrap timber and plywood
- Waterproof wood glue
- Nails: ¾ in
- Wood screws: 8
- Non-toxic paints
- Filler
- Sandpaper
- Woodworking tools

Exploded view

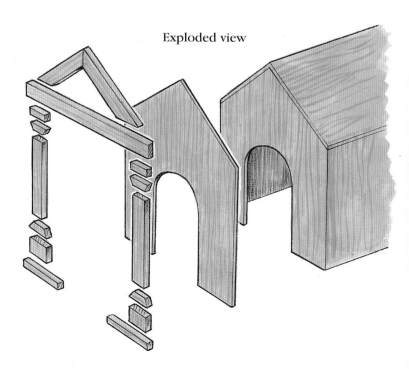

Wooden door handles can be used for decoration

Create dramatic effects with paint or scraps of wood

Dotted line shows outline of kennel behind

Put screws in positions indicated

39

1 Stand the kennel on the plywood and mark the shape of the front, including the door, all round. Draw a second line 1 in. from the first line at the sides and top. Cut out along the outer line.

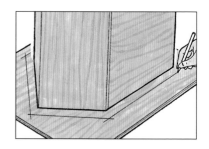

2 Build up the façade before screwing the false front to the kennel. Draw all the features of your design onto the cut plywood.

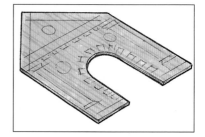

3 Make the roof portico from scrap timber (2 in. x 1 in. is best). Cut the wood to size and glue it to the face of the plywood. Use nails to secure each decorative piece firmly.

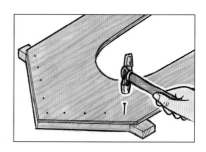

4 Make up the two pillars from 1 in. scrap timber. Measure between the portico and the base to achieve a snug fit. Fix to façade with glue and nails (see step 3).

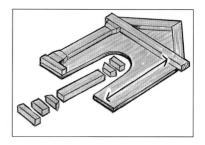

5 To make the decorative brickwork, work out how many bricks you need to suit your size of kennel and cut out the required number from scraps of plywood. Glue them in position on the façade.

6 Drill holes through the façade and screw it to the front of the kennel. Make sure the screws are shorter than the total thickness of wood. Use filler to hide the screw heads, then sand it smooth.
Paint the façade.

Woof-woof Wool Rug

A warm, washable throw to drape the car seats or sofa is a most welcome addition to any pup's possessions. The solicitous owner can make this must-have rug in a moment and thereby guarantee themselves life-long loyalty and gratitude from their dog. Plus, of course, there is the additional boon of hair-free chairs, sofas, and car seats.

Select washable fabrics to complement your dog's coat. The dyed-in-the-wool dog owner may wish to adorn the throw with appliquéd motifs (see pages 58–63) or a spectacular border of blanket stitch in bright-colored thread.

Materials Needed
- Washable velour:
  144 in. x 36 in
- Cotton fabric:
  144 in. x 36 in.
- Embroidery thread
  (optional)
- Basic sewing equipment

42

1 Cut the velour in half to make two pieces, each 72 in. x 36 in. Join, right sides together, along the long edge to make one piece of fabric 72 in. square. Do the same with the cotton fabric.

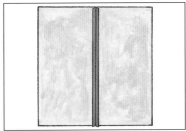

2 Pin the two fabric squares together, right sides facing. Machine stitch around all sides, leaving a gap of 10 in. in one side. Trim corners, then press the seams flat.

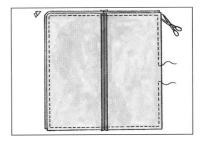

3 Turn right side out, pushing the corners out carefully. Hand or machine stitch the opening closed.

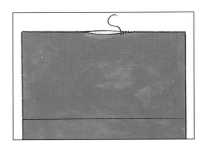

4 Topstitch around all sides 1 in. from the edge. If desired, embroider blanket stitch along the edge of the throw to give a special finish. Or, add appliqué motifs to the cotton side using fusable material (see page 29).

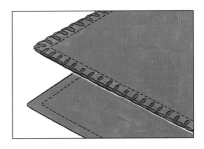

Dog-u-ments

To keep your doggy's paperwork from getting too dog-eared, create an efficient filing system that will simplify both your lives.

This dog-u-ment folder is the ideal solution for storing pedigree certificates, veterinary records, and vaccination details, as well as important mementos and irreplaceable baby puppy photos.

For bonzos with bubbly social lives, add a daily planner.

Materials Needed
- Purchased ring binder
- Colored paper or gift wrap
- Clear plastic pockets
- Sheets of thin poster board
- Adhesive photo corners
- Scissors, ruler, and glue

For Decoration
- Paint and paintbrush
- Stencil board or acetate
- Craft knife
- Cutting mat
- Masking tape
- Ceramic tile or old plate
- Stencil brush

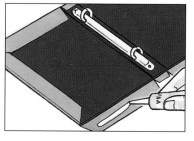

1 Purchase an appropriate gift wrap to cover the binder, or paint or stencil motifs onto plain paper (see pages 58–63). Make sure the paper you decorate is big enough to cover the binder.

2 Cut the decorated paper 1 in. larger than the binder on all sides. Center the binder on the paper. Trim the corners. Turn the edges to the inside of the binder and glue.

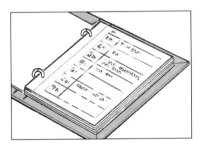

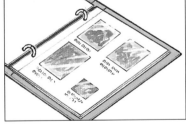

3 Put hole-punched plastic pockets inside to hold documents, certificates, insurance papers, and other vital paperwork.

4 Photographs can be mounted on paper, using adhesive corners to hold them in position. Put them inside plastic pockets for protection.

For Hungry Hounds

While some hungry hounds will eat almost anything, other pooches can be a bit more picky. This mouth-watering array of tasty treats and stylish accessories ensures you will be able to please each and every hound.

Ear-Tidy

Long-eared dogs, such as spaniels, will appreciate the dignity of an ear-tidy to keep their ears from drooping into the food bowl and getting messy. This essential accessory for the long-eared can be made in a snap. But don't let your dog become a fashion victim.

The ear-tidy is strictly for mealtime wear only.

Materials Needed
- Cotton fabric: 12 in. x 4½ in.
- Soft elastic:
  12 in. x 1 in. wide
- Basic sewing equipment

1 Fold the fabric right sides together to make a tube. Stitch along the raw edge with a ¼ in. seam allowance. Press the seam so it is in the center of one side. Turn the tube right side out.

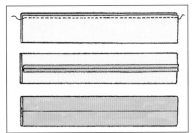

2 Stitch along the length of the fabric tube, ¼ in. from the top and bottom edges.

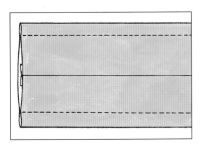

3 Determine the length of elastic that will fit comfortably around your dog's ears. The elastic should be stretched enough to hold the ears up without being tight. Allow a little extra for joining.

4 Thread the elastic through the fabric tube, then sew the ends of the elastic firmly together. Tuck in the raw edges and slipstitch to join the ends of the fabric tube.

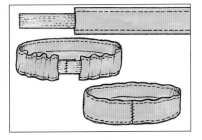

Bowled Over

Every cultured canine appreciates a decorated dish. To embellish your doggy's bowl, paint a design or stencil a motif (see pages 58–63).

Or, letter your dog's name or an appropriate motto such as *cave canum* ("beware of the dog").

1 Select a motif from pages 58–63. Reduce as needed to fit your dog's bowl. Or, draw your own design freehand. To stencil a message, buy an appropriately sized alphabet stencil to use.

2 Cut out the motifs and hold them against the bowl to make sure they fit. Trace the shapes onto stencil board or acetate. Working on a cutting mat, use a craft knife to cut out the shapes.

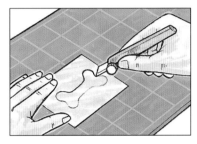

3 Position the stencil on the bowl with masking tape. Apply a thin film of paint to the tile. Holding the stencil brush upright, dab into the paint and then through the stencil onto the bowl.

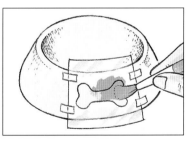

4 Let each motif dry completely before starting work on the next. Dry for several days before filling with dog food. The dishwasher may remove the design, so hand washing is recommended.

Dogs' Dinners

For special times – birthdays, anniversaries, graduations – concoct a robust meal for your darling doggy. These recipes are sure to make tails wag.

Casserole for canines

1 small onion, chopped
1 carrot, chopped
Olive oil
¼ lb mushrooms
1 lb lean beef, cubed
Beef bouillon cube
4 cups water

Fry onion and carrot in a little olive oil until softened, not browned. Place the fried vegetables, the mushrooms, and the meat in a casserole.

Dissolve the bouillon cube in 4 cups of boiling water and add to the casserole.

Place casserole in oven and cook at a medium temperature for two hours.

Allow to cool to room temperature and serve with plain dog biscuits.

Chicken *au Chien*

Most pups go into a wild tail spin for licorice. Given the chance, they'll snatch licorice twists right out of your hand. So treat your dog to this delicious chicken dish, tastefully garnished with licorice-flavored star anise.

You will need:
Chicken pieces
Star anise
Strips of cooked carrots
Potato chips

Cut slits in the raw chicken and push a few star anise flowers inside. Cook chicken pieces in a microwave oven, following the manufacturer's recommended cooking times, or roast in the oven until well done.

Remove any bones, then cut meat into bite-sized pieces. Arrange in the serving dish.

Garnish with a generous bunch of cooked carrot strips. Add a few potato chips to the top – naughty but nice!

Party Snacks

When cooking for family and friends, you might want to prepare something special to keep your wolf at bay – or at least out of the kitchen.

These little treats should be rare indulgences. If your dog gets used to snacks on demand, you'll spend your life in the kitchen and your pet will get too fat. Be sure you keep food refrigerated until you're ready to serve it.

Ready-made Munchies

Quick and easy snacks that your dog is sure to enjoy are available from all good pet stores. While rawhide chewies will keep your pooch occupied for hours, small crunchy biscuits and doggy chocolates will provide only a moment of pleasure. Human snacks, such as potato chips usually prove irresistible to dogs. But certainly cocktail sausages

and cold meats are more nutritious. A *pièce de résistance* for a gourmet dog is a juicy hamburger, still warm and aromatic.

Pooch Pinwheels

Spread a thin slice of wholegrain bread with mashed sardines, a slice of salami, chopped hard-boiled eggs, or mashed tuna mixed with mayonnaise. Carefully roll up the slice of bread, enclosing the filling, then cut across the roll to make savory pinwheels.

Gussied-up Dry Toast

Regular dog biscuits or squares of dried toast can be topped with a choice of goodies for canine parties. Popular toppings are cream cheese, mayonnaise topped with shrimp, smoked salmon spread, and sardines.

Celebration Food Fun

For summer parties, distribute pooch pinwheels in hiding places around the yard. Your pup will have such fun sniffing out these treats that you'll be free to talk to your guests.

Birthday Cake

This yummy cake will be big enough to serve several dogs, so make sure your hound invites friends to the party. Serve up dainty portions to the guests as you won't want to send them home with indigestion. Use dog biscuits for candles and for decorations.

Materials Needed
- 2 large cans dog food
- Bread crumbs
- Milk
- Dog biscuits
- Liver pâté
- Cream cheese
- Piping bag

1 Scoop the meat into a large bowl and mix well with the bread crumbs. Add a little milk. Mold the mixture into a cake shape. Put onto a serving plate.

2 Cover the top with a thin layer of liver pâté. Press bone-shaped biscuits around all sides.

3 If desired, fill a piping bag with cream cheese and write your dog's name or a loving message on top.

4 Decorate with suitably shaped dog biscuits. Keep the cake in the refrigerator until served.

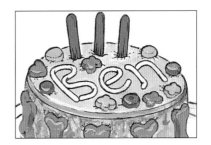

Motifs

The motifs on the following pages have been especially selected for their dog appeal. Check each project to see if you can use the template in the size shown, or if you need to make it bigger or smaller.

Just the right size

If the motif size shown is right for your project, then photocopy or trace it. Cut out the photocopy to create the pattern, or transfer your tracing to thick cardboard or paper before cutting.

Changing sizes

If you want to make your motif bigger or smaller, by far the easiest way is to use a photocopier which can enlarge or reduce the image. If you

don't have access to a photocopier, you will need to use the grid method to alter the size of the motif or pattern.

If you want to make the motifs much smaller, buy some grid paper with divisions as small as an ⅛ in. If you want to make them bigger, buy grid paper divided into 1 in. squares. The grid lines in this book are ½ in. apart.

On your grid paper, roughly sketch in pencil the motif at your chosen size. Now draw the motif much more carefully, copying across the outline square by square. Notice the points where the outline crosses the lines of the original grid. Make sure it crosses the corresponding lines of your own grid.

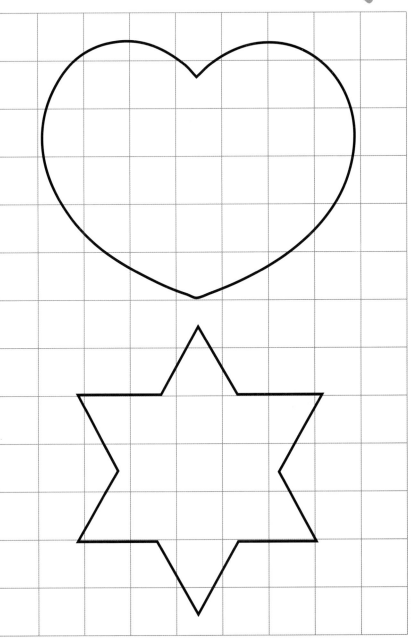

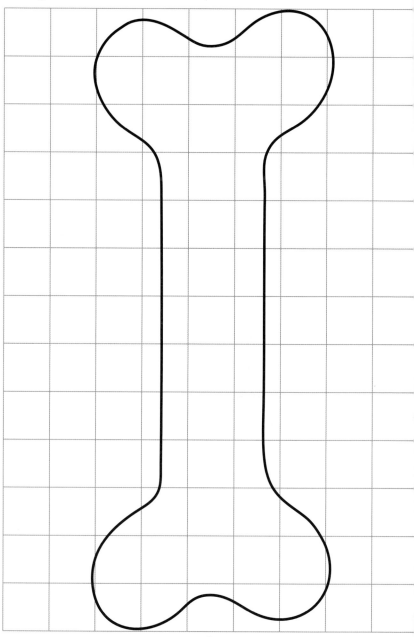

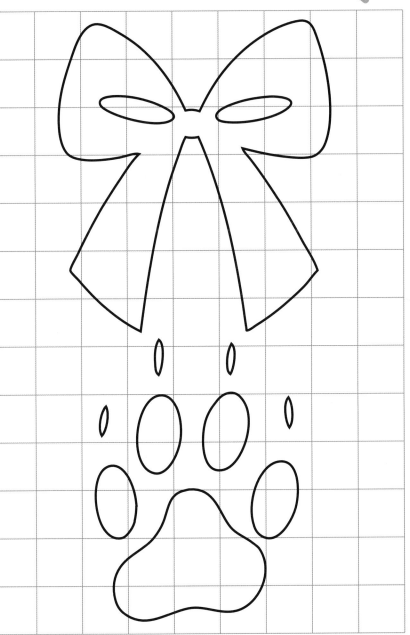

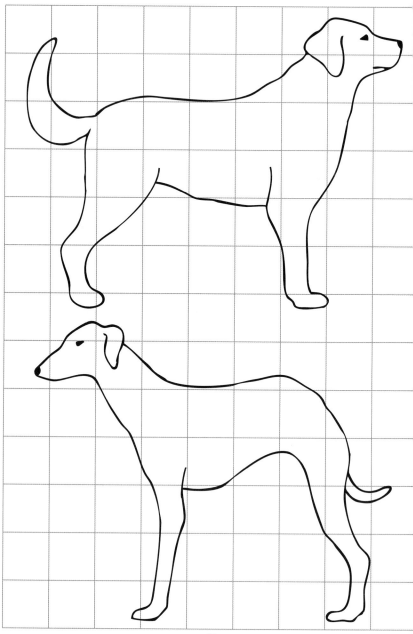

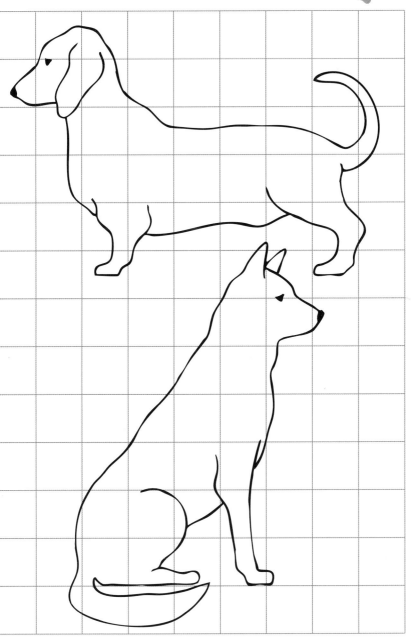

Sewing Notes

All the items in this book have been designed to be quick and easy to make – remember, most dogs are not that demanding. A sewing machine is the easiest way to make the cloth gifts, but they can be made by hand. Use back stitch for hand-sewn seams.

Before you begin a sewing project, you should have the following basic equipment to hand.

BASIC SEWING EQUIPMENT
Scissors
Sewing thread to match fabric
Needles and pins
Thimble (if you use one)
Ruler
Tape measure
Paper and pencil
Tracing paper

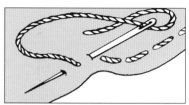
Back stitch

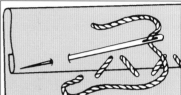
Slipstitch

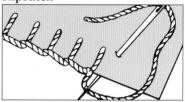
Blanket stitch

Stem stitch

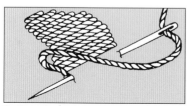
Satin stitch

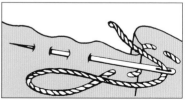
Running stitch